Tupac

by Z.B. Hill

Superstars of Hip-Hop

Tupac

by Z.B. Hill

Mason Crest

Tupac

Mason Crest
370 Reed Road
Broomall, Pennsylvania 19008
www.masoncrest.com

Printed and bound in

First printing
9 8 7 6 5 4 3 2 1

Library of Congress Cataloging-in-Publication Data

Hill, Z. B.
  Tupac / by Z.B. Hill.
     p. cm. – (Superstars of hip-hop)
  Includes index.
  ISBN 978-1-4222-2530-1 (hard cover) – ISBN 978-1-4222-2508-0 (series hardcover) – ISBN 978-1-4222-9232-7 (ebook)
  1. Shakur, Tupac, 1971-1996–Juvenile literature. 2. Rap musicians–United States–Biography–Juvenile literature. I. Title.
  ML3930.S48H55 2012
  782.421649092–dc23
  [B]
                        2011019648

Produced by Harding House Publishing Services, Inc.
www.hardinghousepages.com
Interior Design by MK Bassett-Harvey.
Cover design by Torque Advertising & Design.

Publisher's notes:
• All quotations in this book come from original sources and contain the spelling and grammatical inconsistencies of the original text.
• The Web sites mentioned in this book were active at the time of publication. The publisher is not responsible for Web sites that have changed their addresses or discontinued operation since the date of publication. The publisher will review and update the Web site addresses each time the book is reprinted.

DISCLAIMER: The following story has been thoroughly researched, and to the best of our knowledge, represents a true story. While every possible effort has been made to ensure accuracy, the publisher will not assume liability for damages caused by inaccuracies in the data, and makes no warranty on the accuracy of the information contained herein. This story has not been authorized nor endorsed by Tupac.

Contents

Hip-Hop lingo

Lyrics are the words in a song.

An **album** is a bunch of songs made to go together on a CD.

Rap is a kind of music where rhymes are spoken over music in the background. A **rapper** is a person who rhymes over music, sometimes off the top of his head.

A **recording studio** is a place where musicians go to record their music and turn it into CDs.

A **producer** is the person in charge of putting together songs. A producer makes the big decisions about the music.

A **feud** is a fight between two people or groups that goes for a long time.

When someone is **convicted** of a crime, a judge or a jury decides he is guilty.

Chapter 1

Against the World

In 1994, there was no brighter hip-hop star than Tupac Shakur. He had good looks and talent. His **lyrics** about hard life on city streets gave people hope. He wasn't even twenty-five years old. But already he was many people's hero.

On November 30, 1994, Tupac went to New York City. He was there to help a friend make an **album**. The friend's name was Little Shawn. He was a **rapper**, like Tupac. The two were set to meet at a **recording studio** on Times Square. Tupac was famous. Adding his name to Shawn's album was sure to help it sell better.

Tupac had already created a unique image. He was a rebel. He was a fighter. He rapped about growing up poor and about violence on the streets. He rapped about getting back at people who had hurt him. His music was about his life. It told stories about all the things that had hurt him or made him angry.

Tupac arrived at the Times Square studio around midnight. His sister and a few friends were with him. When he got there, he noticed something. A strange man stood outside the building. The man followed the group as they went inside. In the lobby, Tupac saw two other strange men. And that's when it happened.

All three men pulled guns out at the same time. They ignored the group and went straight for Tupac. They told him to give up his money and jewelry. Instead, Tupac reached for his own gun. When the men saw the gun, they opened fire. Tupac didn't stand a chance. Five shots hit him. Luckily, none of the shots killed him. Then the attackers robbed him. They took about $35,000 worth of jewelry from him.

Only one other person in the group was robbed. The rest were left untouched. Tupac was sure he had been set up.

When armed robbers confronted Tupac in the lobby of Quad Recording Studio in Manhattan, the rapper reached for a concealed gun. Before he could draw the weapon, Tupac was shot 5 times.

Gangsta vs. Gangsta

That same night, in the same building, another rapper was at work. Notorious B.I.G. and **producer** Puff Daddy were recording in an upstairs studio.

Downstairs, the shooting had stopped. Tupac's friends pushed him into the elevator. They wanted to protect him against any further attacks. A few other friends stayed behind to call the police. Tupac was very angry. Still bleeding, he accused everyone of setting him up. He said that lots of people wearing jewelry had been around during the attack. But none of them were robbed. Finally, the ambulance arrived. Tupac went to the hospital. His wounds were treated.

While he healed, Tupac began to track down his attackers. He found out that Notorious "Biggie" B.I.G. had been in the same building on the night of the attack. He also found out that visitors to the building had been buzzed in. This meant that someone on the inside had let the three attackers enter.

But there was a problem. Many people had known about Tupac's arrival that night. Dozens of people might have set him up for the attack. Even so, Tupac accused Biggie of doing it. Biggie denied it, but Tupac was convinced. The two rappers had been friends before. But all that changed. They began a **feud** that would change their lives. Biggie represented the East Coast and Tupac the West Coast.

Against the World

Tupac checked himself out of the hospital. The doctors had done good work on him. His wounds would heal. But he had other problems. He went directly from the hospital to the courthouse. He'd been accused of hurting a woman. He denied it, but he was **convicted** anyway. He was told he had to serve a few years in jail.

Tupac arrives at a New York courthouse on December 1, 1994, the day after being shot. He had checked himself out of the hospital to attend the hearing. The wheelchair-bound rapper was found guilty of sexual assault and sentenced to prison.

While in prison, Tupac released his fourth album, *Me Against the World*. It hit the top of hip-hop charts. It proved that Tupac was a hip-hop star. Not many artists can sell millions of records while in jail!

But Tupac's time in jail only made him more creative, even though he found himself looking into a scary future. While behind bars, he wrote songs called "So Many Tears," "Death Around the Corner," and "If I Die 2Nite." This was a young man who took life seriously.

And yet, no one who knew him would call him a dark or sad person. In fact, they'd say the opposite. Tupac was full of life. He used all of his talents to live and help others live better.

Hip-Hop lingo

A **revolutionary** makes things change, or takes them in a whole new direction.

When a person is **acquitted**, a judge or jury says she is not guilty of a crime.

Inspiration gives someone ideas and makes him want to do something.

A **manager** is someone who helps and guides a musician.

An **audition** is performing for someone to see if that person likes your work and wants to give you a job.

A **roadie** is someone who helps a musician carry his stuff. He sets up his speakers and instruments for him.

A **demo** is a rough, early version of a CD before the real thing comes out.

To **identify** with someone is to see yourself as similar to that person.

Chapter 2

Born Rebel

When he was ten years old, Tupac was living in New York City. A minister asked him what he wanted to be when he grew up. He didn't need to think for very long. "A **revolutionary**," he said. From the beginning, Tupac knew his life would be different from most.

Tupac's mother was born Alice Faye Williams. In the 1960s, she changed her name to Afeni Shakur. She did this as part of her decision to join the Black Panthers.

The Black Panthers were part of the civil rights movement. The goal of civil rights was to make blacks and whites equal. Some groups tried to do this without violence. Others had a different idea about how to achieve this goal. They believed that black people should use violence to get what they wanted. The Black Panthers were one of these groups.

In 1969, Afeni and twenty other Panthers were arrested. They waited for their trial in a New York City jail. While out on bail for several months, Afeni became pregnant. The father was Billy Garland, another Panther member. Afeni and Billy never married. In fact, Billy had no role in raising Tupac. Afeni told Tupac that his father was dead.

On June 16, 1971, in East Harlem, Afeni gave birth to Lesane Parish Crooks. It had only been a month since she had been **acquitted** and released from prison. Afeni had made many enemies while a Panther. She gave Tupac a false name to keep people from hurting him. Later on, she changed his name to Tupac Amaru Shakur. The name was taken from Túpac Amaru II, who was a revolutionary in Peru during the 1780s. Tupac was born to be a fighter.

Tupac poses with a toy gun in a photo taken during the late 1970s. His half-sister Sekyiwa is on the right, wearing a pink coat. The Shakur family had little money, and moved often as Afeni tried to earn a living.

Growing Up

Afeni Shakur had a hard time finding a job. Not many people wanted to hire someone who had been a Black Panther. This meant the young family was often poor. Things only got worse when Afeni had another baby. Tupac soon had a half-sister named Sekyiwa.

Meanwhile, Tupac was growing up. When he was twelve, his mom put him in a local theater group. Within a year, he got a major part in a play called *A Raisin in the Sun*. It told the story of a black family. Tupac played the son of a man who thinks money is happiness. The play was performed at the Apollo Theater in Harlem. This was a famous theater. It was a big deal for the young man.

In 1985, the family moved to Baltimore, Maryland. The move was another big break for Tupac. He was accepted into the Baltimore School for the Arts (BSA). This was truly the beginning of Tupac's career. It was here that he learned how to be an artist. He wrote poetry, studied dance—even ballet!—and acted in many plays. The stage was also Tupac's chance to start rapping. He wrote rhymes and performed them for his classmates.

Tupac met one of his best friends at BSA. Her name was Jada Pinkett. She was a young student studying drama. She would go on to be a movie star. Jada and Tupac both came from troubled homes. They both grew up poor. They each wanted to use their talents to break out of ghetto life. They quickly became close friends. Jada told Michael Eric Dyson what Tupac was like in those days. She said, "He was poor. I mean, when I met Tupac, and this is not an exaggeration, he owned two pairs of pants, and two sweaters. Okay? He slept on a mattress with no sheets when I went to his room, and it took me a long time to get into his house because he was embarrassed. He didn't know where his meals were coming from."

Life in the Jungle

Things weren't going so well for Tupac's mother. She started using crack cocaine. This led to constant fighting between mother and son. Tupac could not accept her behavior. He became very angry. Sometimes he yelled at people. Jada Pinkett said, "He was really rough on Afeni. And you know, he took every opportunity to punish anybody who he felt didn't do right by him, by his standards. That came from his relationship with Afeni. . . . Your mother is your pulse to the world. And if that pulse ain't right, ain't much else going to be right."

The time finally came to move again. The violence in their neighborhood worried Afeni. She put Tupac and Sekyiwa on a bus and sent them to Marin City, California, to live with a friend. Even though he would only live there for a few years, Marin City shaped much of Tupac's life. Marin City turned out to be an even worse ghetto than the one in Baltimore. Eventually, Afeni joined her family in Marin City. She found a new home for them. Their new house was in a rough Marin City neighborhood called the "Jungle."

Tupac didn't live with Afeni much longer. Her drug habit had grown worse. And he never felt accepted in the Jungle. People made fun of him for his shabby clothes. He didn't play basketball like most of the other boys his age. He was often beat up by gang members.

He went to high school for a while. His teachers admired his acting ability. But he lost interest and dropped out at age seventeen. He moved in with some friends. He got a job delivering pizzas. He and his roommates formed a rap group, called the One Nation Emcees.

While attending the Baltimore School for the Arts, Tupac became friends with another talented young performer, Jada Pinkett. At the school, Jada studied dance and choreography. She later pursued an acting career, appearing in such films as *Menace II Society* and *Set It Off*.

When Tupac was about 17, he and his sister moved from Baltimore to California. The Shakurs settled in a tough neighborhood of Marin City nicknamed the Jungle. Many of Tupac's lyrics draw on his experiences in the ghetto of Marin City.

It was here that Tupac found his voice as a rapper. He drew **inspiration** from the streets. Tupac was part of a hip-hop movement called "gangsta rap." Tupac told KMEL radio about how he and his friends made music. He said, "[They were] just giving truth to the music. Being in Marin City was like a small town, so it taught me to be more straightforward with my style. . . . I was encouraged to go straight at it and hit it dead on and not waste time trying to cover things. In Marin City, everything was straightforward. Poverty was straightforward. There was no way to say 'I'm poor,' but to say, 'I'm poor.'"

Many Talents

Tupac was a young man with many talents.

One day, Tupac was rhyming out loud in a San Francisco park. He came across a woman named Leila Steinberg. She was reading an interesting book, and they started to talk about it. Leila knew the hip-hop world. She **managed** a few young rappers already. When she heard Tupac rap, she asked him to meet one of her friends, Atron Gregory. Gregory was the manager of a rap group called The Digital Underground. Leila gave Tupac the chance to **audition** for Gregory.

Tupac blew Gregory away. He was so impressed, he offered him a job on the spot. He told Tupac he'd have to start as a dancer and a **roadie**. But he promised he'd be rapping eventually.

Tupac couldn't wait forever, though. So in the meantime he made a few **demos**. He was still hoping to get a record deal for a solo album. He also auditioned for a movie called *Juice*. At the time, Tupac didn't think he stood a chance. But the movie producer loved him. He gave Tupac a lead role! Tupac had an energy that viewers liked.

In 1992, Tupac appeared in *Juice*, a feature film about the lives of four young men growing up in Harlem. The low-budget movie was a financial success, earning more than $20 million, and many critics praised Tupac's performance.

Juice tells the story of three young people caught up in a murder. Tupac played Bishop, one of the meanest characters. And yet, because of his skill as an actor, people couldn't help but love Bishop. The director of *Thug Immortal* said, "There was something special about him. You saw it in his records. I saw it a little bit more in his movies. He had that glow. He had that charisma. There was no one else who looked like him. He had the eyebrows. He had the cheekbones. You know, handsome."

The movie had been filmed in New York City. When Tupac returned to California, he was famous. Thousands of people had seen *Juice*. Suddenly Tupac was a movie star! But he kept his sights set on the rap game. When he got back, Atron Gregory finally got him a deal with Interscope Records. This was it. This was Tupac's big chance. In 1991, he came out with his first album, *2pacalypse Now*.

Tupac told the stories he always wanted to tell. *2pacalypse* told about life on the streets. It painted a picture of pain. It gave hope to those still living in the ghetto. Some hip-hop artists spend their whole lives trying to get out of poverty. Once they're out, they often rap about how rich or how famous they are. Right from the start, Tupac was different. He did become rich and famous, but he still **identified** with the people in the ghetto. He didn't forget them.

Tupac's star was on the rise. The only question now was—where would he go next?

Hip-Hop lingo

An album goes **platinum** when it sells more than 1,000,000 copies.
An album goes **gold** when it sells more than 500,000 copies.

Chapter 3

Living the Gangsta Life

Fame came quickly—but so did trouble. Tupac kept getting in fights.

Tupac had been cast for the movie *Menace II Society*. But then he was fired. Later that year, Tupac ran into the men who had fired him from the movie. He got in a fight with them.

No one knows for sure what made Tupac such a troublemaker. He had a lot of chances to change his ways. But he kept making one mistake after another. He had a lot of anger inside him.

Keep on Rising Higher

But all the trouble seemed to make Tupac rap even better. His second album was a huge success. It quickly went **platinum**, reaching millions of fans.

The album told stories of urban struggle. One song, "Keep Ya Head Up," was written for black women. It urged fans to give women respect. It stood out from many hip-hop songs that say bad things about women.

Other songs blamed the police for not behaving well. One song, "The Streetz R Death Row," talks about how hard life is for many young urban blacks. It talks about crime, drugs, and broken homes.

In 1994, Tupac formed a rap group called Thug Life. The group gave Tupac a chance to team up with friends. Thug Life's lyrics were so violent that no one wanted to release their first album. They had to tone down the violence before Interscope agreed to produce it. Their first album ended up being called *Thug Life: Vol. 1*. It quickly went **gold**.

Prison Days

Then Tupac's life took another strange turn. He and a few other men were accused of a terrible crime against a woman. Tupac claimed he didn't hurt her. But he was convicted anyway. He had to serve between one-and-a-half to four-and-half years in prison.

In some ways, prison turned out to be good for Tupac. He decided to make his life better. He read a lot of books. He told visitors he wanted to give up the thug life. One of his visitors was his old friend, Jada Pinkett. Author Michael Dyson wrote that Tupac told Jada his plans after prison. "I'm going to stop thugging," he said. "I am getting rid of the guns. . . . I'm changing, Jada. I don't want to do this rap thing anymore. I'm just going to act."

But things didn't work out that way. Tupac had another visitor while in jail. The man's name was Marion "Suge" Knight. He was head of Death Row Records. His label's specialty was gangsta rap. Tupac was gangsta rap's biggest star, and Suge wanted to have him on his team.

Tupac was broke. He'd earned millions of dollars from his three albums and movies. But he couldn't save any of it. He lost a lot to court dealings and lawyers. Suge made Tupac a deal: sign with

Tupac Shakur spits at reporters after leaving a New York courthouse in July 1994. Durig the mid-1990s, despite his great success, the rapper had a series of run-ins with the law, and spent some time in prison.

Death Row, and Suge would pay Tupac's bills. It was too good to refuse. Author Cathy Scott says that Tupac answered, "I want to join the family. Just get me out." And just like that, Tupac was back on the gangsta rap scene.

Marion "Suge" Knight, head of Death Row Records, had a reputation as a dangerous and ruthless man. In 1995 he promised to help get Tupac out of prison if the rapper would make albums for Death Row.

A Dangerous Man

Suge's nickname is short for "Sugar Bear." Suge played college football. He even went pro for a short time. But he gave up football to be a bodyguard for a musician. From there, Suge began building his recording label from the bottom up.

Suge Knight had a bad reputation. He hung around a lot of tough guys and thugs. He called his label Death Row because most of the people who worked there had been in prison. What's more, Suge was said to have close contact with a dangerous gang, the Bloods. He surrounded himself with the gang's color—red. He drove red cars, wore red suits, and even painted his swimming pool's walls red.

Suge was also a good businessman. He had a limo waiting for Tupac the day he left prison. It took him straight to a private jet, which flew him across the country to L.A. That night, Tupac stepped into Death Row's studio.

Within a few months, Tupac made *All Eyez On Me*. It was a hit for Death Row. And it was one of the best albums Tupac ever made.

All Eyez On Me sold more than 7 million copies. Tupac now had close ties to Death Row Records. Many Death Row artists were guests on the album. These included Snoop Dogg, Method Man, and Dr. Dre. Tupac found himself a bigger and bigger player on the Death Row team.

Silver Screen

Tupac was back. His time in prison made him hungry for more than music. He wanted to act again, too. In 1993, he'd starred in a movie called *Poetic Justice*. Once again, Tupac chose a movie a lot like his music. It told the story of poor people trying to escape the ghetto. Tupac's character, Lucky, stays away from gangs. But he must make money working a job that he hates.

WE DONE DONE IT AGAIN

Tupac Amaru Shakur 1971-1996 R. I. P.

2PAC

THUG HOLIDAY

Another Tribute to Hip-Hop's Most Influential MC

SUGE KNIGHT Remembers his soldier
SHOCK-G The man who put him on
ATLANTA SHOOTOUT Two cops got bucked

PLUS: KHIA ★ ANGIE MARTINEZ ★ CLIPSE

Tupac Shakur remains incredibly popular, and articles about him or trubutes to his music continue to appear in hip-hop publications. In polls done by MTV (2003) and *Vibe* magazine (2004), hip-hop fans rated Tupac the greatest MC of all time.

In 1996, Tupac made two more movies. The first was called *Bullet*. Tupac played a drug dealer in it. The next was called *Gridlock'd*. Tupac played a drug addict trying to kick his habit. Film reviewer Roger Ebert called *Gridlock'd* Tupac's best performance.

Sadly, the young man would never get to build on his amazing talent as an actor. *Gridlock'd* would be the last movie Tupac would ever make.

Hip-Hop lingo

The **media** is the group of people who create news. Media can be photographs, videos, or news articles.

A **fundraiser** raises money to help people.

The **Crips** are a famous gang. Their enemy was another gang, called the Bloods.

Chapter 4

East Coast vs. West Coast

Many people today have heard of the famous "East Coast–West Coast" feud. A lot of work has gone into finding out exactly what caused it. But one thing's for certain: Tupac was very much involved.

The East Coast Stars

In 1993, a young producer named Sean "Puffy" Combs created his own label. He called it Bad Boy Entertainment. Bad Boy got its big break when it signed Notorious B.I.G. The rapper also went by Biggie Smalls (or just Biggie). In 1994, Biggie made a hit album. He called it *Ready to Die*.

Biggie was a six-foot-two-inch, 300-pound rapper from New York City. Like Tupac, he was very talented. But Suge Knight thought he sounded a little too much like Tupac. He claimed that Combs and Biggie had ripped off their sound from Death Row. Things only got worse from there. Fights broke out between rappers from both crews. A few times, Biggie and Tupac were personally involved.

Much of the time, however, fights were between other members of the two labels. The head of Def Jam records was a man named

Russell Simmons. He explained what was really going on to *Spin* magazine. He said, "The war was created and fueled by our own radio stations and our own [hip-hop] magazines." The so-called "war" was really just a few arguments. It was not as big a problem as the **media** made it seem.

Tupac (left) poses with Snoop Dogg (center) and Suge Knight (right) for a promotional photo. As one of Death Row's biggest stars, Tupac was drawn into a bitter feud between Knight and Sean "Puffy" Combs, the head of East Coast-based Bad Boy Entertainment.

Bad Boy Entertainment CEO Sean Combs (left) is pictured with former Def Jam Records executive Russell Simmons in a 2002 photo. Combs attempted to downplay the East Coast-West Coast rivalry, but was unable to prevent the war of words from turning violent.

A Sudden Ending

All of this led to the night of September 7, 1996. The scene was Las Vegas, Nevada. Suge Knight had invited Tupac to a boxing match at the MGM Grand Hotel. The two men planned to go to an after-party at Club 662. The party was a **fundraiser** for kids.

Notorious B.I.G. emerged as a star on the hip-hop scene with the release of his first album, *Ready to Die*, in 1994. The rivalry between Biggie and Tupac grew more bitter throughout 1995, as each rapper insulted the other in his lyrics.

The first warning sign came as they left the MGM. Two of Tupac's bodyguards noticed a man named Orlando Anderson. He was a member of a rival gang, the **Crips**. Tupac and two bodyguards attacked him. Suge broke up the fight, and everyone left the hotel. Suge and Tupac got into a sleek BMW. The bodyguards followed in another car. They were headed for the party at Club 662.

It was a hot night. Both Suge and Tupac had rolled their windows down. Hip-hop blasted on the car stereo. Then the car rolled to a stop at a red light. While they waited for the light to turn green, a Cadillac pulled up beside them. Inside were three or four men. Suddenly, one of them stuck a gun out the window. He fired thirteen shots.

Tupac tried to dive into the backseat. But his seatbelt held him tight. He was hit three times. Somehow, Suge wasn't hit.

Suge asked Tupac, "You hit?"

"I'm hit," Tupac answered.

As the Cadillac drove away, Suge went into action. "You need a hospital, Pac. I'm gonna get you to a hospital right now." He put the BMW into gear and hit the gas.

But he didn't get far. Two shots had hit the BMW's tires. The Las Vegas streets were packed with traffic. Suge tried to steer over curbs and around cars. But the odds were against him. The police followed Suge's BMW. They didn't know yet what had happened. They thought Suge was the bad guy.

It took a few minutes for the police to understand that Suge was innocent. By now, Tupac's shirt was soaked in blood. Suge and a bodyguard lifted Tupac out of the car. When he arrived at the hospital, he was unconscious. He stayed alive for six days. And then he died. He was just twenty-five years old.

Chapter 5

Life After Death

His life ended, but his music didn't. Tupac has made more money after death than he did while he was alive. Tupac recorded dozens of songs before he died. Some say he made three songs in a single day. These songs were released after he died.

In 1996, Death Row put out a new Tupac album. It was just a few weeks after Tupac's death. They called it *Makaveli: The Don Killuminati: The 7 Day Theory*. The album sparked rumors about Tupac's death. Some said Tupac faked his death. They said he was living under a different name. They took the letters in the album title and mixed them up. They made them spell the sentence, "Ok on the 7th u think I'm dead, yet I'm really alive." Other people had different ideas. Some said they heard the words "Suge shot me" on the first track.

Before he died, Tupac also filmed a video for his song "I Ain't Mad at Cha." The video showed him being shot and killed. Next, it showed him floating up to heaven. Some people made a big deal of these things. Others said that Tupac's death was sad, but not unexpected. He lived in a violent world and died a violent death.

Murders Never Solved

Tupac's murder was never solved. Biggie was also later shot, but before his death, he said he had nothing to do with Tupac's death. Then in 2002, a writer for the *L.A. Times* said Biggie had wanted Tupac dead. When the article came out, Biggie's family was upset. They said, "This false story is a disrespect to not only our family but the family of Tupac Shakur. Both men will have no peace as long as stories such as these continue to be written."

A *Rolling Stone* writer had another idea about the deaths. He said that Suge Knight was behind both killings. Suge said this idea was totally false. Nothing has ever linked him to the murders.

Mothers in Action

Biggie's mother is Voletta Wallace. Since her son's death, she's worked constantly to find his murderer.

But Afeni Shakur took a different path. "Not even a nanosecond have I concerned myself with who shot him or why they shot him, or what should happen to them," she told the Associated Press. "I spend my time putting my son's work out, because, guess what— they shot him, but did not shut him up."

Afeni has put her energy into Tupac's music. She has worked hard to get his music out to the fans. Since his death, his albums have sold tens of millions of copies. Afeni has tried to show a different side of her son. In 2004, Afeni released *Loyal to the Game*. It was Tupac's ninth album since his death. *Loyal* has many songs of hope and love.

Afeni insists she has a job to do. She wants to carry out what she saw as her son's mission. She says that Tupac wanted to give back to others. So she founded the Tupac Amaru Shakur Center for the Arts. It's in Stone Mountain, Georgia. It helps young kids who want to be performers. It has classes in creative writing, voice, act-

After Tupac's death, Afeni Shakur won control of most of her son's un-released music, and formed a music label to oversee the production of posthumous albums. Since 1996, numerous albums of his music have been officially released.

A bronze statue of the rapper stands in the Peace Garden at the Tupac Amaru Shakur Center for the Arts in Atlanta. "Every generation picks their own heroes," sculptor Tina Allen said at the unveiling ceremony. "This generation's hero is clearly Tupac Shakur."

ing, stage and set design, and poetry. It truly seems like something Tupac would have loved to do. As a young man, his dreams began in an arts school in Baltimore. Now, maybe some other young person will find the same dream in Tupac's school.

Afeni doesn't seem to be slowing down anytime soon. She told the Associated Press about her passion. "We have a list of things that Tupac left for us to do, so all we're doing is going over that list, going down that list, checking them off. So, at the end of the day, we'll be able to say we've done fulfilled our responsibility to an incredible human being."

Tupac's life was filled with trouble. He made lots of bad decisions. But he was a talented artist, with lots to offer the world. Now, the best parts of Tupac continue to live. He's finally getting the chance to make the world a better place for kids like him.

Time Line

1971 Lesane Parish Crooks is born on June 16 in New York City; his mother, Afeni Shakur, soon changes his name to Tupac Amaru Shakur.

1983 Twelve-year-old Tupac appears in the play *A Raisin in the Sun* at the Apollo Theater in Harlem, New York.

1985 Afeni Shakur moves her family to Baltimore, where Tupac enrolls as a student at the Baltimore School for the Arts.

1988 Fearing violence in the family's Baltimore neighborhood, Afeni Shakur sends her son across country to live with friends in Marin City, California.

1989 While rapping in a San Francisco park, Tupac meets Leila Steinberg, who is impressed with his talent and introduces him to rap promoter Atron Gregory.

1990 Tupac joins the rap group Digital Underground as a dancer and roadie, but is soon given the chance to rap with the group.

1991 Tupac's first solo album, *2Pacalypse Now*, is released and soars to the top of the hip-hop charts.

1992 Tupac makes his screen-acting debut by playing a leading role in the film *Juice*.

1993 Tupac's second album, *Strictly 4 My N.I.G.G.A.Z.* released; meanwhile, his trouble with the law begins when he is charged in Michigan for assaulting another rapper with a baseball bat. Tupac is also accused of sexual assault by a New York woman.

1994 In November, Tupac is shot five times while entering the lobby of a recording studio in New York; he survives the shooting and leaves the hospital early so that he may hear the verdict in the sex assault case. He is convicted.

1995 In February, Tupac begins serving his sentence in prison on the sexual assault conviction. He is granted early parole in October through the intercession of Death Row Records founder Marion "Suge" Knight, who signs him to a recording contract.

1996 His first Death Row album, *All Eyez on Me*, is released and goes platinum. On September 7, Tupac and Suge Knight are ambushed in their car on a Las Vegas street. Tupac dies a week later.

1997 Afeni Shakur founds the Tupac Amaru Foundation to provide education in the arts for young people; Suge Knight begins a five-year jail term for his role in the assault on Orlando Anderson, a member of the Crips street gang; Biggie Smalls is murdered on a Los Angeles street.

2001 *Rolling Stone* publishes a story suggesting that Suge Knight had Tupac murdered to avoid paying the rapper a $3 million debt.

2002 *The Los Angeles Times* publishes a series of series alleging that Biggie Smalls paid $1 million to Orlando Anderson to kill Tupac.

2003 The documentary *Tupac: Resurrection*, narrated in Tupac's voice, is released.

2004 *Loyal to the Game* released by Amaru Records, the record label started by Afeni Shakur to produce her son's music.

2005 *The Rose, Volume 2*, an album featuring Tupac's poetry set to music, is released.

2005 *Tupac: Resurrection* is nominated for an Academy Award as Best Documentary.

2012 A projection of Tupac performs with Dr. Dre and Snoop Dogg.

In Books

Baker, Soren. *The History of Rap and Hip Hop*. San Diego, Calif.: Lucent, 2006.

Comissiong, Solomon W. F. *How Jamal Discovered Hip-Hop Culture*. New York: Xlibris, 2008.

Cornish, Melanie. *The History of Hip Hop*. New York: Crabtree, 2009.

Czekaj, Jef. *Hip and Hop, Don't Stop!* New York: Hyperion, 2010.

Haskins, Jim. *One Nation Under a Groove: Rap Music and Its Roots*. New York: Jump at the Sun, 2000.

Hatch, Thomas. *A History of Hip-Hop: The Roots of Rap*. Portsmouth, N.H.: Red Bricklearning, 2005.

Websites

Death Row Records
www.deathrowmusic.com

Official Tupac Fan Site
www.hitemup.com

Official Tupac Forum
2pacshakur.forum.st

Tupac Amaru Shakur Foundation
www.tasf.org

Tupac on MTV
www.mtv.com/music/artist/2pac/artist.jhtml

Discography

1991   2Pacalypse

1993   Strictly 4 My N.I.G.G.A.Z.

1994   Thug Life: Thug Life Vol. 1

1995   Me Against the World

1996   All Eyez on Me

Released After Death

1996   Makaveli: The Don Killuminati: 7 Day Theory

1997   R U Still Down

1998   2Pac's Greatest Hits

1999   Still I Rise

2000   The Rose that Grew from Concrete

2001   Until the End of Time

2002   Better Dayz

2003   Tupac: Resurrection

2004   Loyal to the Game

2005   The Rose, Volume 2

2006   Pac's Life

Index

About the Author

Z.B. Hill is a an author and publicist living in Binghamton, New York. He has a special interest in adolescent education and how music can be used in the classroom.

Picture Credits

1: Dreamstime, Lawrence Agron
6: Zuma Press/Michel Haddi/eyevine
8: UPI/Jim Ruymen
10: KRT/David Handschuh
12: Paramount/Everrett Collection
14: WENN
17: WENN
18: Paramount/Everrett Collection
20: Paramount/Everrett Collection
22: UPI/Chi Modu
25: AP Photo/Bebeto Matthews
26: KRT/Chuck Fadely
28: NMI/Mechell Feng
30: Zuma Press/Michel Haddi/eyevine
32: NMI/Death Row Records
33: Zuma Press/NYPP
34: KRT/Death Row Records
36: NMI/Paramount Pictures
39: Zuma Press/Rena Durham
40: PRNews Foto/NMI

To the best knowledge of the publisher, all other images are in the public domain. If any image has been inadvertently uncredited, please notify Harding House Publishing Services, Vestal, New York 13850, so that rectification can be made for future printings.